The

4th

Day

The 4th Day

Bishop Dr. Apostle Zella Berry Case

2020

All Biblical References taken from the King James Version of the Holy Bible.

Publisher: Bishop Dr. Apostle Zella Berry Case.
Distributor: LuLu.com.

Contact Information: www.drzellaberrycase.com.
Email: zellacase@mebtel.net

Dedication

To Eric & Starr

My Beloved Children

Time and time again I have dreamed and thought about the measures that Christ goes through in His word to assist us in understanding of who He is and why He does things in the way that He presents them to us. Often its simple things. Sometimes its things that have hidden meanings which can baffle the very elect, "saints."

Sometimes He does things just to let us know that He is the only one that can bring peace, joy, and hope. Sometimes He delivers and sometimes He doesn't. Sometimes He makes us wait on a request for Him to do something for us and sometimes He shows up immediately. Sometimes He wants us to report blessings that He gives known and sometimes He says to "tell no one what He did for us." (Mark 1:40-45)

"When he was come down from the mountain, great multitudes followed him. And behold, there came a leper and worshipped him, saying, Lord, if thou wilt, thou canst make me clean. And Jesus put forth his hand, and touched him, saying, I will; be thou clean. And immediately his leprosy was cleansed. And Jesus saith unto him, See thou tell no man; but go thy way, shew thyself to the priest, and offer the gift that Moses commanded, for a testimony unto them."

Sometimes Jesus says no. You see my friends, as Christians we are surrounded with many struggles from our daily experiences, including not only our needs, but those needs that are around us, which are great. We cannot meet every need, just some of them. Really we cannot meet any need without the assistance from the Holy Spirit.

Jesus does understand that we as humans are limited and we cannot be everywhere that there is a need, nor can we do anything about some of the needs that we are aware of except to pray. We have limited strength and limited resources. We should always know that Jesus is the one that we can call upon to assist us when we have done all that we can do to rectify the situation.

Sometimes even those of us with the best intentions have to say *"no"* when it is not possible to do something for someone that is in need. But then, is it always wrong to say *"no"* when there is need?

It is a true fact, Jesus was quite generous with His time, attention, and resources. We too are told to be rich in mercy and kindness, expansive in our charity and to be willing to forsake everything to follow Christ. But for limited human beings, often with many obligations, are there no limits? Of course, there have to be. But, we all at times have asked ourselves when needs arise, "What would Jesus Do?" Did He ever say, *"No?"* Of course, there were times when Christ said, "no." Yet, I am sure that when He said "no" there wasn't anyone that wanted to hear that answer. We want to hear "yes" all the time, especially when we are in trouble and have exalted all of our resources and energy.

We want Jesus to come to our rescue. Right now, in a hurry, but...often we have to wait. I believe that it is in those times, that is, the times of waiting that is, is when we develop our spiritual muscles. It is in those times of waiting I believe that our faith in Christ is formed not on our behalf but for the glory of Christ. Why am I saying that?

All of us who believe on Christ must realize early in our quest in following Him to know without a shadow of a doubt that following Him is about believing that He makes no mistakes and that we can take Him at His word. This includes knowing that what He promises, what He always does is for our best and that He will get the credit for whatever is done for the good and permitted when things don't go good, which I believe is used for our good and for our trust and faith in Him.

This book entails a story, a true story found in the Bible about a friend of Jesus, actually a family of friends that had seen Jesus perform miracles, healings, and wonders many times, and at this specific time in their lives request His presence in a miraculous way, you could say it was an emergency, but Jesus did not show up when requested.

`As the storyline goes, the family requested for Jesus to come to see about a family member that was sick unto "death." Yet, Jesus tarries and the family member died.

Most people with a general understanding of the Bible know that the first four books of the New Testament are called the Gospels. Most people also understand on a broad level that in the Gospels each tell the story of Jesus Christ, that is, His birth, ministry, teachings, miracles, death, and resurrection.

What many people don't know, however, is that there's a striking different audience in all of the Gospels. Now the first three Gospels, I am referring to Matthew, Mark, and Luke, are known together as the Synoptic Gospels. Now for the Gospel of John which happens to be so unique that 90% of the material it contains regarding Jesus' life cannot be found in the other Gospels.

Let me explain those statements made above deeper in their perspectives. Jesus speaks in long, soaring soliloquies in the Gospel of John. The parable-centric teacher of the synoptics disappears and is replaced by one who engages in extended dialogues with individuals and long, theologically heavy monologues. In a typical Bible, this can be seen by the large blocks of red text in comparison to the synoptics.

Differences Between the Gospel of John and the Synoptic Gospels

The gospel according to John is very different than the other three gospels, which are commonly known as the

Synoptic gospels, Matthew, Mark, and Luke. In other words we must identify who the audience of each gospel is speaking to and speaking from.

Many will counter with this argument: "Well, the Apostle John (according to tradition) wrote it, and he was actually there." These folks forget, however, as can be seen in the lists of disciples from the synoptics in point "B" below that Matthew was also a disciple, and according to tradition, he wrote Matthew. One very important difference is also the style.

In the synoptic gospels, Jesus teaches primarily in *short sayings* and *parables*. In John, we find neither of these; instead, we find long monologues. There are fewer "signs" in John as well. On top of that, many "details" are quite different:

a) In the Synoptics, Jesus does not begin His ministry until John is imprisoned (Mark 1:14). John 3:24 shows their ministries overlapping.

b) Disciples vary

- Mark 3:16 So he appointed the twelve: Simon (to whom he gave the name Peter); James son of Zebedee and John the brother of James (to whom he gave the name Boanerges, that is,

Sons of Thunder); and Andrew, and Philip, and Bartholomew, and Matthew, and Thomas, and James son of Alphaeus, and Thaddaeus, and Simon the Cananaean, and Judas Iscariot, who betrayed him.

- Matthew 10:2 These are the names of the twelve apostles: first, Simon, also known as Peter, and his brother Andrew; James son of Zebedee, and his brother John; Philip and Bartholomew; Thomas and Matthew the tax collector; James son of Alphaeus, and Thaddaeus; Simon the Cananaean, and Judas Iscariot, the one who betrayed him.
- Luke 6:14 Simon, whom he named Peter, and his brother Andrew, and James, and John, and Philip, and Bartholomew, and Matthew, and Thomas, and James son of Alphaeus, and Simon, who was called the Zealot, and Judas son of James, and Judas Iscariot, who became a traitor.

c) John has no list of all 12, and he never names the John the Apostle, the 2 James, Levi / Matthew, Thaddaeus, Bartholomew, or 1 Simon (not Peter). However, he does add Nathaniel. C. John's Gospel notes 3 Passovers. So, if you take him literally and chronologically (which I don't think we should do – that's not John's point), then Jesus' ministry is about 3 years. For the Synoptics, it appears to only be **one year** as only one Passover is noted.

d) John 13-17, though definitely the "Last Supper," is not a Passover Meal. John 18:28 makes clear that the Passover meal is to be eaten the evening after Jesus is crucified (compare that to Mark 14:12-18, which makes clear that Jesus did eat the Passover, so he was crucified the day after).

e) According to the stories of the "Garden of Gethsemane" in the Synoptics, Jesus says something to the effect of "Abba, Father, for you all things are possible; remove this cup from me; yet, not what I want, but what you want," as is seen in Mark 14:36. Compare these passages from John that seem to remove any semblance of asking that the cup be removed:

"Now my soul is troubled. And what should I say— 'Father, save me from this hour?'; No, it is for this reason that I have come to this hour."

John 12:27

"Am I not to drink the cup that the Father has given me?"

John 18:11b

f) In John, Jesus carries the cross by himself (John 19:17) but in the synoptics, Simon of Cyrene carries the cross.

g) In John, Jesus is crucified sometime AFTER noon (John 19:14). Mark 15:25 says it has happened by 9a.m.

h) John 20:19-23 has a completely different understanding of how the disciples receive the Holy Spirit than the book of Acts does. For John, Jesus breathes the Holy Spirit on them. For Acts, they are told to go to Jerusalem and wait for it to come AFTER Jesus has already ascended. Either John disagrees with Acts' understanding, or he has never heard Acts' version.

Yes, there happens to be major, yet similarities found in the Gospel of John and the Synoptic Gospels. All four Gospels are complementary, and all four tell the same basic story about Jesus Christ. But there's no denying that John's Gospel is quite different from the other three in both tone and content. The big question is *why?* Why would John have written a record of Jesus' life that is so different from the other three Gospels? And what does this have to do with this author's writing of this book entitled, "The 4th day?" Anytime Christ does anything He wants us to take a careful examination of the "HOW, WHEN, WHY, and for WHAT PURPOSE!

When looking at all the gospels we must look at their audience as previously stated, in whom they are addressing. For this book the author uses the Apostle John for his uniqueness among the Gospels and his purposes and theme. But prior to looking at John's gospel let me briefly explain and explored each Gospel writer and how they viewed Christ' ministry.

For example, the Gospel of Mark was written primarily for the purpose of communicating Jesus' story to a generation of Gentile Christians who had not been eyewitnesses to the events of Jesus' life. For that reason, one of the main themes of the Gospel is the identification of Jesus as the "Son of God" (Mark 1:1; 15:39). Mark wanted to show a new generation of Christians that Jesus really was the Lord and Savior of all, despite the fact that He was no longer physically on the scene.

The Gospel of Mathew was written with both a different purpose and a different audience in mind. Specifically, Matthew's Gospel was addressed primarily to a Jewish audience in the 1st century which is a fact that makes perfect sense given that a large percentage of the early converts to Christianity were Jewish. One of the major themes of Matthew's Gospel is the connection between Jesus and the Old Testament prophecies and predictions regarding the Messiah. Essentially, Matthew was writing to prove that Jesus was the Messiah and that the Jewish authorities of Jesus' day had rejected Him.

Like Mark, the Gospel of Luke was originally intended primarily for a Gentile audience because the author himself was a Gentile. Luke wrote his Gospel with the purpose of providing a historically accurate and reliable account of Jesus' birth, life, ministry, death, and resurrection (Luke 1:1-4). In many ways, while Mark and Matthew sought to form Jesus' story for a specific audience (Gentile and Jews, respectively), Luke's purposes were more remorseful in nature. He wanted to prove that Jesus' story was true.

The writers of the Synoptic Gospels sought to solidify Jesus' story in a historical and apologetic sense. The generation that had witnessed Jesus' story was dying off, and the writers wanted to lend credibility and staying power to the foundation of the fledgling church, especially since, prior to the fall of Jerusalem in A.D. 70, the church still existed largely in the shadow of Jerusalem and the Jewish faith.

The major purposes and themes of John's Gospel were different, which helps to explain the uniqueness of John's text. Specifically, John wrote his Gospel after the fall of Jerusalem. That means he wrote to a culture in which Christians experienced severe persecution not only at the hands of Jewish authorities but the might of the Roman Empire, as well.

The fall of Jerusalem and the scattering of the church was likely one of the spurs that caused John to finally record his Gospel. Because the Jews had become scattered and disillusioned after the destruction of the temple, John saw an evangelistic opportunity to help many see that Jesus was the

Messiah and therefore the fulfillment of both the temple and the sacrificial system (John 2:18-22; 4:21-24).

The uniqueness of John's Gospel also is concerned with the different ways each Gospel writer focused specifically on the person and work of Jesus Christ.

In Mark's Gospel, for example, Jesus is portrayed primarily as the authoritative, miracle-working Son of God. Mark wanted to establish Jesus' identity within the framework of a new generation of disciples.

In Matthew's Gospel, Jesus is portrayed as the fulfillment of the Old Testament Law and prophecies. Matthew takes great pains to express Jesus not simply as the Messiah prophesied in the Old Testament but also as the new Moses, the new Abraham, and the descendant of David's royal line (remember Matthew begins with the lineage of David who is a descendant of Christ).

While Matthew focused on Jesus' role as the long-expected salvation of the Jewish people, Luke's Gospel emphasized Jesus role as Savior of all peoples. Therefore, Luke intentionally connects Jesus with a number of outcasts in the society of His day, including women, the poor, the sick, the demon-possessed, and more. Luke portrays Jesus not only as the powerful Messiah but also as a divine friend of sinners who came expressly to "seek and save the lost."

Additionally, in the midst of the previously stated information, and prior to talking about the significance for this book the author wants you to know that John's Gospel is a thorough exploration of Jesus Himself.

Indeed, it's interesting to note that while the term *"kingdom"* which is spoken by Jesus 47 times in Matthew, 18 times in Mark, and 37 times in Luke, it is only mentioned 5 times by Jesus in the Gospel of John. At the same time, while Jesus utters the pronoun *"I"* only 17 times in Matthew, 9 times in Mark, and 10 times in Luke, He says *"I"* 118 times in John. The Book of John is all about Jesus explaining His own nature and purpose in the world. Isn't that amazing?

Now let us look at this dramatic storyline found in the Bible and view some additional information concerning this storyline than the one that you might have heard about Lazarus's death and raising by Christ and ultimately what happened and what this story refers to and questions within even today. The event takes place and is seen in the gospel of John chapter 11.

"Now a certain man was sick, named Lazarus, of Bethany, the town of Mary and her sister Martha. (It was that Mary which anointed the Lord with ointment, and wiped his feet with her hair, whose brother Lazarus was sick.) Therefore his sisters sent unto him, saying, Lord, behold, he whom thou lovest is sick. When Jesus heard that, he said, This sickness is not unto death, but for the glory of God, that the Son of God might be glorified thereby. Now Jesus loved Martha, and her sister, and Lazarus. When he had heard therefore that he was sick, he abode two days still in the same place where he was. Then after that saith he to his disciples, Let us go into Judaea again. His disciples say unto him, Master, the Jews of late sought to stone thee; and goest thou thither again? Jesus answered, Are there not twelve hours in the day? If any man walk in the day, he stumbleth not, because he seeth the light of this world. But if a man walk in the night, he stumbleth, because there is no light in him. These things said he: and after that he saith unto them, Our friend Lazarus sleepeth; but I go, that I may awake him out of sleep. Then said his disciples, Lord, if he sleep, he shall do well. Howbeit Jesus spake of his death: but they thought that he had spoken of taking of rest in sleep. Then said Jesus unto them plainly, Lazarus is

dead. And I am glad for your sakes that I was not there, to the intent ye may believe; nevertheless let us go unto him. Then said Thomas, which is called Didymus, unto his fellow disciples, Let us also go, that we may die with him. Then when Jesus came, he found that he had lain in the grave four days already. Now Bethany was nigh unto Jerusalem, about fifteen furlongs off: And many of the Jews came to Martha and Mary, to comfort them concerning their brother. Then Martha, as soon as she heard that Jesus was coming, went and met him: but Mary sat still in the house. Then said Martha unto Jesus, Lord, if thou hadst been here, my brother had not died. But I know, that even now, whatsoever thou wilt ask of God, God will give it thee. Jesus saith unto her, Thy brother shall rise again. Martha saith unto him, I know that he shall rise again in the resurrection at the last day. Jesus said unto her, I am the resurrection, and the life: he that believeth in me, though he were dead, yet shall he live: And whosoever liveth and believeth in me shall never die. Believest thou this? She saith unto him, Yea, Lord: I believe that thou art the Christ, the Son of God, which should come into the world. And when she had so said, she went her way, and called Mary her sister secretly, saying, The Master is come, and calleth for thee. As soon as she heard that, she arose quickly, and came unto him. Now Jesus was not yet come into the town, but was in that place where Martha met him. The Jews then which were with her in the house, and comforted her, when they saw Mary, that she rose up hastily and went out, followed her, saying, She goeth unto the grave to weep there. Then when Mary was come where Jesus was, and saw him, she fell down at his feet, saying unto him, Lord, if thou hadst been here, my brother had not died. When Jesus therefore saw her weeping, and the Jews also weeping which came with her, he groaned in the spirit, and was troubled. And said, Where have ye laid him? They said unto him, Lord, come and see. Jesus wept. Then said the Jews, Behold how he loved him! And some of them said, Could not this man, which opened the eyes of the blind, have caused that even this man should not have died? Jesus therefore again groaning in himself cometh to the grave. It was a cave, and a stone lay upon it. Jesus said, Take ye away the stone. Martha, the sister of him that was dead, saith unto him, Lord, by this time he stinketh: for he hath been dead four days. Jesus saith unto her, Said I not unto thee, that, if thou wouldest believe, thou shouldest see the glory of God? Then they took away the stone from the place where the dead was laid. And Jesus lifted up his eyes, and said, Father, I thank thee that thou hast heard me. And I knew that thou hearest me always: but because of the people which stand by I said it, that they may believe that thou hast sent me. And when he thus had spoken, he cried with a loud voice, Lazarus, come forth. And he that was dead came forth, bound hand and foot with graveclothes: and his face was bound about with a napkin. Jesus saith unto them, Loose him, and let him go. Then many of the Jews which came to Mary, and had seen the things which Jesus did, believed on him. But some of them went their ways to the Pharisees, and told them what things Jesus had done. Then gathered the chief priests and the Pharisees a council, and said, What do we? for this man doeth many miracles. If we let him thus alone, all men will believe on him: and the Romans shall come and take away both our place and nation. And one of them, named Caiaphas, being the high priest that same year, said unto them, Ye know nothing at all, Nor consider that it is expedient for us, that one man should die for the people, and that the whole nation perish not. And this spake he not of himself: but being high priest that year, he prophesied that Jesus should die for that nation; And not for that nation only, but that also he should gather together in one the children of God that were scattered abroad. Then from that day forth they took counsel together for to put him to death. Jesus therefore walked no more openly among the Jews; but went thence unto a country near to the wilderness, into a city called Ephraim, and there continued with his disciples. And the Jews' passover was nigh at hand: and many went out of the country up to Jerusalem before the passover, to purify themselves. Then sought they for Jesus, and spake among themselves, as they stood in the temple, What think ye, that he will not come to the feast? Now both the chief priests and the Pharisees had given a commandment, that, if any man knew where he were, he should shew it, that they might take him.

Just a bit of HISTORY to further assist you.

Prior to this event Jesus had performed many miracles. He performed twenty-eight miracles prior to raises Lazarus from the dead. He had:

The Miracles of Jesus prior to raising Lazarus from the dead

1. Jesus changed water into wine (John 2:1-11).

2. Jesus cured the nobleman's son (John 4:46-47).
3. The great catch of fishes (Luke 5:1-11).
4. Jesus cast out an unclean spirit (Mark 1:23-28).
5. Jesus cured Peter's mother-in-law of a fever (Mark 1:30-31).
6. Jesus healed a leper (Mark 1:40-45).
7. Jesus healed the centurion's servant (Matthew 8:5-13).
8. Jesus raised the widow's son from the dead (Luke 7:11-18).
9. Jesus stilled the storm (Matthew 8:23-27).
10. Jesus cured two demoniacs (Matthew 8:28-34).
11. Jesus cured the paralytic (Matthew 9:1-8).
12. Jesus raised the ruler's daughter from the dead (Matthew 9:18-26).
13. Jesus cured a woman of an issue of blood (Luke 8:43-48).
14. Jesus opened the eyes of two blind men (Matthew 9:27-31).
15. Jesus loosened the tongue of a man who could not speak (Matthew 9:32-33).
16. Jesus healed an invalid man at the pool called Bethesda (John 5:1-9).

17. Jesus restored a withered hand (Matthew 12:10-13).
18. Jesus cured a demon-possessed man (Matthew 12:22).
19. Jesus fed at least five thousand people (Matthew 14:15-21).
20. Jesus healed a woman of Canaan (Matthew 15:22-28).
21. Jesus cured a deaf and mute man (Mark 7:31-37).
22. Jesus fed at least four thousand people (Matthew 15:32-39).
23. Jesus opened the eyes of a blind man (Mark 8:22-26).
24. Jesus cured a boy who was plagued by a demon (Matthew 17:14-21).
25. Jesus opened the eyes of a man born blind (John 9:1-38).
26. Jesus cured a woman who had been afflicted eighteen years (Luke 13:10-17).
27. Jesus cured a man of dropsy (Luke 14:1-4).
28. Jesus cleansed ten lepers (Luke 17:11-19).

Now Jesus was often doing things for the "good" of mankind on what the Jewish religious community considered *"not good,"* as it relates to miracles because performing miracles was considered *"work."*

In actuality He performed seven (7) miracles on the sabbath. The Sabbath was meant to be a day in which worship was not for healing and for *"Doing good,."*

Listed below are those miracles:

1. Jesus Heals a Lame Man by the Pool of Bethesda - (John 5:1-18.)
2. Jesus Drives Out an Evil Spirit - (Mark 1:21-28.)
3. Jesus Heals Peter's Mother-in-law - (Mark 1:29-31.)
4. Jesus Heals a Man with a Deformed Hand. (Mark 10:14.)
5. Jesus Heals a Man Born Blind - (John 9:1-16.)
6. Jesus Heals a Crippled Woman - (Luke 13:10-17.)
7. Jesus Heals a Man with Dropsy - (Luke 14:1-6.)

Jesus is Lord of the Sabbath and that makes the Sabbath the true ***"Lord's Day."*** In performing these seven Sabbath miracles, Jesus is showing us how to keep the Sabbath. He emphasized the humane element of mercy, compassion, and loving-kindness by healing and *"doing good"* on the Sabbath. He showed us that we are not to be *"hard hearted"* as the Pharisees were when it comes to the Sabbath. Yes, we as

Christians are supposed to worship Christ on the Sabbath Day because it is God's day. Doing works for Him and witnessing to others is a form of worship. Worship isn't just singing songs to Him but also sharing His word and doing works that justify Him.

So why was it so wrong to Heal on the Sabbath in those days?

By history, the Jews had a **law** that they were trying not to break the Sabbath because earlier, they had disobeyed God by worshiping idols and God had put them in captivity for 70 years. (Look at this, another use of the number SEVEN 7).

"Wherefore I caused them to go forth out of the land of Egypt and brought them into the wilderness. And I gave them my statutes, and showed them my judgements, which if a man do he shall even live in them. Moreover, also I have gave hem my sabbaths, to be a sign between me and them, that they might know that I am the LORD that sanctify them. But the house of Israel rebelled against me in the wilderness: they walked not in my statutes, and they despised my judgments, which if a man do, he shall even

live in them; and my sabbaths they greatly polluted: then I said, I would pour out my fury upon them in the wilderness, to consume them. But I wrought for my name's sake, that it should not be polluted before the heathen, in whose sight I brought them out."

Ezekiel 20:19-14

Therefore, anytime someone did work on the Sabbath, the Jews looked down on the person and they were taken to the Pharisees to be punished. Healing, carrying your bed, and walking more than a Sabbath's day journey was forbidden.

All the information that I have given you thus far is really to assist you in the understanding of the Triune Godheads that always will work together and fit jointly in all their motives and attributes. What am I saying? Look at how many miracles that He (Jesus) performed and compare it to how many years He lived on Earth.

John Chapter 11 – the story

Mark was not an original disciple of Christ. Luke was not an original disciple of Christ. Matthew was and so was John. Just thought I would mention that. So, John the writer of the Gospel of John, 1st, 2nd, and 3rd John, and Revelation is who the author uses for this book and for one of the subject of this book, as we concentrate on the 4th day.

When reading Chapter 11 of John you will discover that Jesus loved Mary, Martha, and Lazarus. What's more the family knew that Jesus loved them! So, when Lazarus fell sick, the sisters sent word to Jesus. Because of the close relationship they shared with Jesus, they referred to Lazarus as the *one whom Jesus loves*, in the message that they sent to Jesus. It is obvious that they expected Jesus to rush to their aid and heal their sick brother, because of the loving relationship that this family shared with Jesus.

Who would not expect that to happen? Jesus was and is a compassionate person, a servant, a healer, a deliver, the Savior, the Messiah, the sustainer of the word, why would He not come to the assistance of a friend in need. A friend who is sick unto death. A friend that He loved like a brother. WHY, WHY, WHY?

Often Jesus has used close relationships with people that He loved to prove a point. This storyline is one of those cases.

Jesus had visited the three siblings, Mary, Martha, and Lazarus many times and had broken bread with them. Even when the messenger comes to Jesus and requested that He come to see about Lazarus, he says: "the one that you love is ill." Therefore, we must come to the conclusion that there was a wonderful relationship with the siblings and Jesus loved them and seemingly would do what they requested because of His love. But…

When Jesus received the invitation, the messenger told Jesus that Lazarus, "He whom you love is ill." This phrase, "He whom you love," is significant. Yes, Jesus loved all he came in contact with, but the words hints at how Jesus and Lazarus were true friends, and not just acquainted. You understand, we all have friends that we care deeply about and wish and pray that they do well in life, but then we have one or two friends that we love deeply and are like sisters or brothers – even closer than a sister or brother.

Jesus took this opportunity to let not only the crowd who seemingly was mourning the death of Lazarus, He took this opportunity to show the entire community that He was not only a healer, but He also had the power to raise the dead after so many days. I will discuss that later.

The delay

To our human minds this delay of Jesus coming to see about Lazarus might seem strange, uncaring, but remember Jesus was God in the flesh, incarnate and knew Lazarus's life span.

Jesus took His time before leaving for Bethany, knowing that the Jewish culture deemed a person dead after three days. So, was He waiting so that those around Lazarus would have no doubt that their friend was gone? Sometimes Christ does things to point us in another direction and possibly assist us in knowing what we believe and in whom we believer – that is truly believe in when the going gets tough.

After announcing His friend was dead, Jesus arrived at Martha and Mary's house and by this time the women's brother had been dead for four days. Martha seemingly chastised Jesus, telling Him that her brother wouldn't have died if He had come sooner. Now, I am sure she loved her brother dearly, but Martha was fretting over another issue. What was that issue?

The Issue

You see the economic structure of ancient Jewish culture, Martha and her sister Mary probably were not permitted to earn a living and need their brother's financial support, and now his support was gone because he was dead. This was a crisis, a catastrophe on many levels for them to lose Lazarus.

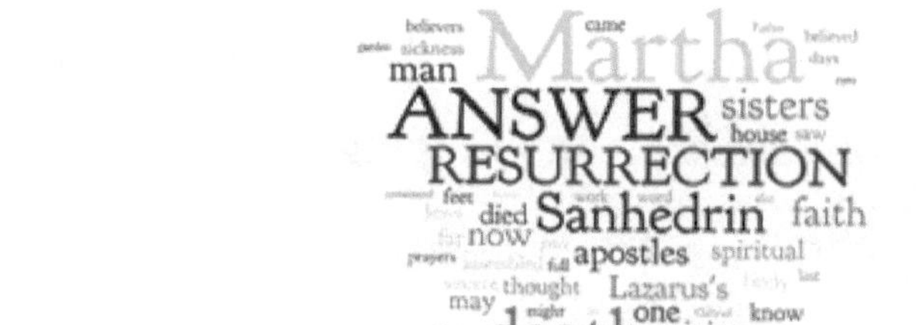

Lazarus was such a great friend to Jesus that He stood at his grave and wept. Can you imagine that? Jesus, God in the flesh weeping. It is therefore difficult to understand why Jesus seems to give such a lukewarm response, when He received the news that Lazarus was sick. If Jesus truly loved this family, then shouldn't He have rushed to their aid and healed Lazarus, when the family needed His help the most? Or shouldn't Jesus have spoken the Word from where He was and healed Lazarus even at a distance, just like He had healed the centurion's servant from a distance? (Matthew 8:5–13). Or perhaps like how He had healed the nobleman's son? (John 4:49–53). Why did not Jesus do anything like that for Lazarus? Some would wonder, ***"Perhaps Jesus did not love Lazarus enough."*** Did Jesus intentionally delay returning to heal Lazarus, so that He could perform the greater miracle of raising a dead Lazarus? Did Jesus intentionally let Lazarus die, when He could have easily saved him? John states that before the Lazarus incident Jesus had escaped from the hands of the Jews who were trying to kill Him and had gone to the place beyond the Jordan where John the Baptist used to baptize i.e. Bethabara. But do these doubtful questions hold water?

Now these are reasonable doubts, but we are here to see whether they hold water, and to see whether we can find the true reason why Jesus delayed going to Bethany.

Did Jesus intentionally let Lazarus die, when He could have saved him?

Now Lazarus and his family lived in Bethany. When the news of Lazarus sickness reached Jesus, Jesus was at the place called Bethabara as Scripture states which is beyond the Jordan. The distance between Bethany and Bethabara is around 15 to 20 miles, i.e. a day's journey. After receiving the news Jesus stayed there two (2) more days before returning. When Jesus reached Bethany, He was told that it had been four (4) days since Lazarus died. Let us trace the chain of events systematically albeit backwards.

1. Day three (4) since Lazarus died. - Jesus makes the one (1) day journey from Bethabara to Bethany, i.e. around (twenty)**20** miles and raises Lazarus.
2. Day three (3) since Lazarus died. - Jesus spends day two (2) of two (2) days at Bethabara.
3. Day two (2) since Lazarus died. - Jesus spends day one (1) of two (2) days at Bethabara.
4. Day one (1) since Lazarus died. - Jesus receives news about Lazarus's sickness. Messengers take at least one (1) day to make the around **20** mile journey and to find Jesus.
5. Day Lazarus died. - Messengers depart to find Jesus to tell Him about Lazarus sickness. Lazarus probably dies soon after they depart and is buried the same day.

Therefore, by tracing this chain of events we see that Lazarus probably died almost immediately after or in the very least on the very same day the messengers left to find Jesus, and was buried the very same day, as per Jewish regulations. Therefore, when the messengers reached Jesus at Bethabara the next day, Lazarus had already died the previous day itself. *It is therefore impossible to support the claim that Jesus intentionally let Lazarus die, just so that He could perform the miracle of raising him from the dead.* Because when Jesus received the message of Lazarus's sickness, Lazarus was already dead and buried! Remember Jesus is God in the flesh who knows all and sees all and that includes the time of our birth and the time of our death.

This actually helps us to understand why Jesus would wait at Bethabara for two more days even after receiving the urgent summons.

Whatever happened, it turns out that Jesus had reached Bethany just in time. It was 4 days since Lazarus was buried, and if there was a good time to perform the miracle of raising Lazarus from the dead, it was now.

A Jewish Belief about the dead

According to Jewish belief the soul of the departed person hung around the body for three (3) days after it's death. The soul would depart after three (3) days and then the body would start decaying. If the raising was performed within those three (3) days, the Jews would have claimed that there was no miracle involved, as the spirit had simply returned to the body within the requisite time. By the time Jesus reached Bethany, four (4) days had passed, and the body had started decomposing, evident by the *stink* referenced.

By performing the miracle on the ***4th day*** after Lazarus death and burial, Jesus was demonstrating His power and authority over **death** itself, that even a dead person could be raised from the grave, even after rot and decomposition had set in the body, by His express command.

Did Jesus not love this family?

The tender dialogues between Jesus and the sisters we see in this chapter, we see that Jesus did love this family intimately, and so it was not a lack of love, that delayed the coming of Jesus.

Was Jesus afraid of the Jews?

If the gospel accounts are to believed, it was quite the opposite. Jesus knew why He had come to planet Earth, and that was to die for the sins of mankind, so that those who accepted His sacrifice would be forgiven and justified in

God's sight. So He knew where His path would lead Him, and He was aware that it would cost Him His very life.

Was Jesus trying to show off His miraculous powers?

On contrary, the gospels show that all that Jesus did was for the glory of God. What do we get out of this? We read in Hebrews that Jesus prayed for deliverance from the cup of suffering He was about to endure. And while God didn't immediately answer His prayer, God did raise Him from the dead three (3) days after His death. Maybe it is too late for us, but for God it is never too late.

These are dangerous times to be a Christian. Sometimes it may seem that God is absent when we need God the most. When we are overcome and we need God to act, God is conspicuously absent. And while we wait for hope, we grow old and withered and finally depart on that lonely bleak journey to the opposite shore after death, and all light and joy and hope is extinguished. It may be too late for us now. But its never too late for God.

"Behold, I tell you a mystery: We shall not all sleep, but we shall all be changed — in a moment, in the twinkling of an eye, at the last trumpet. For the trumpet will sound, and the

dead will be raised incorruptible, and we shall be changed. For this corruptible must put on incorruption, and this mortal must *put on immortality. So when this corruptible has put on incorruption, and this mortal has put on immortality, then shall be brought to pass the saying that is written: "Death is swallowed up in victory. O Death, where* is *your sting?*
O Hades, where is *your victory?"*
1st Corinthians 15:51–55

Remember in this storyline Mary and Martha's brother, Lazarus, became sick. His sickness was obviously quite serious, or else they would not have sent for Jesus to heal him. Jesus, who knows all things, clearly knew that Lazarus would die if He did not heal him. Jesus chose not to heal him for one clear reason: **so that God and His Son would be glorified, and so that the disciples would believe in Him.**

Although Lazarus clearly died because of his sickness, the reason his sickness was not to *"end in death"* was because Jesus knew what He was going to do. It was God's will that Lazarus would die from this sickness so that Jesus would raise him up from the grave. In so doing, God and His

Son would be glorified, and the miracle would cause the disciples to believe in who Jesus was.

We see something similar in John 9 when Jesus heals the blind man. Scripture says he was *born* blind that works of God may be displayed in him. In this example (and others), we are made aware of God's complete sovereignty over our lives. Jeremiah 18 describes Israel as clay in the potter's (God's) hands, which is echoed in Romans 9. The Lord has complete control over our lives, including even being able to raise us from the dead.

As we read a little further we see how Lazarus is raised, John 11:38-46:

"So Jesus, again being deeply moved within, came to the tomb. Now it was a cave, and a stone was lying against it. Jesus said, Remove the stone. Martha, the sister of the deceased, said to Him, Lord, by this time there will be a stench, for he has been dead four days. Jesus said to her, Did I not say to you that if you believe, you will see the glory of God? So they removed the stone. Then Jesus raised His eyes, and said, Father, I thank You that You have heard Me. I knew that You always hear Me; but because of the people standing around I said it, so that they may believe that You sent Me. When He had said these things, He cried

out with a loud voice, Lazarus, come forth. The man who had died came forth, bound hand and foot with wrappings, and his face was wrapped around with a cloth. Jesus said to them, "Unbind him, and let him go. Therefore many of the Jews who came to Mary, and saw what He had done, believed in Him. But some of them went to the Pharisees and told them the things which Jesus had done."

Many believe and I do too that if Jesus had not said "Lazarus come forth!", but only said "Come forth!", then all the dead would have arisen!

Earlier before this miracle Jesus had healed people on the Sabbath. It was the Sabbath when Jesus healed the man who was blind since birth. As had happened before, this healing on the Sabbath raised the ire of religious leaders to a fevered pitch. Additionally, Jesus taught plainly on this occasion that He was the Son of God. Ultimately, there was a call for His life among the leading Jews for uttering such "blasphemy" (John 10:33). Therefore, no matter how much *"good"* Jesus did He was a target. So, He was in danger, and that danger was real.

At the 4th day after Lazarus had died

On the fourth day, “the drop of gall, which had fallen from the sword of the “angel” and caused death, and it was then working its effect, and that, as the face changed, the soul took its final leave from the resting-place of the body.”[1]

Even so, Jesus asked to be directed to the place of burial. Once there, He commanded that the stone covering the entrance to the tomb be removed. Martha warned that the decaying body of Lazarus would likely stink, but Jesus was not swayed (John 11:39). The stone was moved, and after Jesus prayed He “cried with a loud voice, Lazarus, come forth” (John 11:43). The spirit of Lazarus returned to his body, “and he that was dead came forth, bound hand and foot with graveclothes: and his face was bound about with a napkin. Jesus saith unto them, Loose him, and let him go” (John 11:44).

Two-Fold Sign of authority

As related by John “the beloved,” the purpose of this sign of power was at least twofold.

1. First, it deepened the faith and belief in Christ held by the disciples (John 11:15, 45).

2. Second, this miracle allowed the disciples to see the glory of God through Jesus's power over death (John 11:40). Furthermore, it is interesting that the name Lazarus means **"helped of God."** This sign communicated our outright dependence upon Christ. He alone is our sole source of lasting help when facing death.

John carefully described Lazarus exiting the tomb wrapped in His burial clothing.

"And he that was dead came forth, bound hand and foot with graveclothes: and his face was bound about with a napkin. Jesus saith unto them, Loose him, and let him go."
John 11:44

Literally, this image communicates that Lazarus was actually dead and properly buried, he even had the napkins still on his face. Lazarus had no ability within himself to rise from the dead, or even to free himself from the constraints of the grave clothes.

John makes clear to us that both Lazarus and Jesus were buried according to current custom. Their dead bodies had been wrapped in strips of cloth and there was another cloth that covered the face and held the mouth closed. But there is a difference in the two stories.

After Lazarus was raised to life, he came out of the tomb wrapped up in the linens. He had to be released from the grave clothes that still bound him. That was not the case with Jesus. He left his grave clothes behind in the tomb, they did not restrain him. Figuratively, it conveys to the reader that he meaning Lazarus was not leaving death behind permanently but would one day be dressed in grave clothes a second time.

Lazarus came back to life, but it was the same type of life he had before. His body would be subject to dying again one day. That is not the case with Jesus. His body passed through death and would never die again. Jesus' resurrected body was not restricted by walls or grave clothes, he passed right through them.

When Christ was resurrected, John carefully describes how Jesus's burial clothes were left in the tomb, and His napkin left in the tomb – to say I will return. (This was actually a custom in that day that when the man of the house left the dinner table and was not finish eating, he would leave his napkin on the table or plate of food to say, I will return to finish what I began). Jesus is returning and He will not ever again die since He had conquered death (John 20:6–8).[2]

So, the empty grave clothes point to the fact that Jesus' resurrection is a new thing. Others had been raised from the dead in Jesus' ministry and even in the ministry of some Old Testament prophets. But those people all died again. Even though others were raised from the dead previously, Jesus is the *firstborn* from the dead (Colossians 1:18). He is the first of the new creation, the first to pass through death to a life that is no longer under the constraints or the threat of death. And as the first, he makes it possible for many others to follow, all who trust Him for salvation.

This miracle of Lazarus being raised from the dead after the **fourth** day shows that Christ possessed power over death. When He (Christ) cause the man born blind to get his sight and in the case of Lazarus, brought life to a dead man, if taken together, Jesus is the light and the life of the world.[3] Because Lazarus was raised from the dead, we know more securely that death (as well as life) is part of the stewardship of Christ.

Passing out of this life and into the next is not a random action dictated by statistical probability. Quite the opposite, for we can establish deeper faith through experiences with death, and we may detect the glory of God couched in the encounter as well.

Finally, the words of Jesus to Martha on this occasion,

"I am the resurrection, and the life: he that believeth in me, though he were dead, yet shall he live: and whosoever liveth and believeth in me shall never die."
John 11:25–26

indicates that Jesus had power not only to raise Lazarus from the dead in an instant but also to resurrect him for eternity.

This is a beautiful picture of the resurrection that all believers will ultimately experience the power of God. As our Lord says, he who believes in Him will live, even if he dies. Just as we are bound by sin while we are spiritually dead, once God gives us faith and causes us to be spiritually born *("born again"),* God unbinds the chords of sin that ensnare us. It is in this sense that when Jesus says when the Son sets you free, you are free indeed (John 8:36).

Like Lazarus, we have a resurrection to which we can look forward. While Lazarus' resurrection in John 11 was temporary (Lazarus eventually died), our resurrection will be with a new body.

Yes, we will lose this mortal, perishable body and put on an immortal, imperishable body. This will happen because death has been conquered by our great God and Savior, Jesus Christ. May we bring glory to Him until then, and forever more.

Others raised from the dead

The Scriptures had already recorded that both Elijah and Elisha was raised from the dead. However, Jesus raising Lazarus from the dead after the **fourth** day in the grave was truly a miracle. The Pharisees and teachers of the Law had pursued Jesus for a sign to prove Him as Messiah to the people and the nation. Although He rebukes their request in dismay, Jesus does actually say that a sign will be given to them in a particular form.

"Then some of the scribes and Pharisees answered him, saying, "Teacher, we wish to see a sign from you." But he answered them, "An evil and adulterous generation seeks for a sign, but no sign will be given to it except the sign of the prophet Jonah. For just as Jonah was three days and three nights in the belly of the great fish, so will the Son of Man be three days and three nights in the heart of the earth. The men of Nineveh will rise up at the judgment with

this generation and condemn it, for they repented at the preaching of Jonah, and behold, something greater than Jonah is here. The queen of the South will rise up at the judgment with this generation and condemn it, for she came from the ends of the earth to hear the wisdom of Solomon, and behold, something greater than Solomon is here."
Matt 12:38-42

Another common belief was that on the **fourth** day, people believed that the spirit left the body and went to Sheol or Hades, and there was no hope for life without a miracle. By the **fourth** day in Israel's hot climate, advanced decay would be destroying the body and the stench would have been overwhelming. When Jesus called Lazarus to life from the dead and healed his rotted corpse, the people knew that He was the true Messiah, performing genuine miracles as the prophets had foretold!

As the sub-topic above says, there were others and at other times in the Bible, in the Old Testament who had died and in this particular case the family was on their way to bury a man and the body of the dead person touched the bones – meaning the body of the dead was decomposed, the dead man which was being funeralized was raised. Look at this: It was the bones of Elisha.

After Elisha the prophet died, he was buried in a cave or tomb. Moabite raiders attacked Israel every spring, one time interrupting a funeral. Fearing for their own lives, the burial party quickly threw the body into the first convenient place, Elisha's tomb. As soon as the body touched Elisha's bones, the dead man came to life and stood up on his feet. Evidently the men who tossed the body in Elisha's tomb observed the man raised from the dead and spread the story far and wide.

"So Elisha died, and they buried him. Now bands of Moabites used to invade the land in the spring of the year. And as a man was being buried, behold, a marauding band was seen and the man was thrown into the grave of Elisha, and as soon as the man touched the bones of Elisha, he revived and stood on his feet."

2nd Kings 13:20-21

What in the world? Elisha was dead. And yet when a corpse was thrown into his tomb hastily in an attempt to hide from marauding bands of Moabites, the man came back to life simply by his corpse touching Elisha's bones. Even as miracles go, that one's quite impressive.

Yet it's not one we tend to talk about all that often. Elisha and the widow's oil, Elisha raising the Shunammite's son, Elisha sending Naaman the leper to dip in the Jordan: these we know and love. We might even be quite familiar with the floating axe-head, the feeding of the one hundred, or the healing of the water. But yet there seems to be a silence cast over Elisha's bones and the raising of the dead man.

Now, I imagine that silence is due to a certain discomfort. Why?

We shouldn't be uncomfortable to talk about this story, for there is much we can learn from Elisha's bones. The Holy Spirit did not inspire this verse to have us hastily rush past it in the most hushed of tones.

"Scripture does not say that that dead man was brought to the tomb of Elisha with the aim and purpose that he might be brought back to life by contact with his bones, as though it had been at that time the custom among the people of God to run to the sepulchres of the prophets or saints in order to seek grace and power among the bones of the dead by means of vows and invocations. But the text says that that man was by an unexpected emergency cast into the sepulchre of Elisha when they wanted to bury him and, because the brigands came upon them, did not have time to make a grave. Therefore, lest the unburied corpse should be exposed to the caprice of the enemies, the opened the cover of the sepulchre that was nearest, which was that of Elisha, and did not lay the dead person in it (for they did not have time for that), but threw in the corpse. When it had fallen to the bottom, it touched the bones of Elisha and came back to life …

Now , also after that miracle took place, we do not read that the bones of Elisha were taken out of the tomb, elevated to a high place, carried about; they were not set forth to be kissed, touched, viewed; they were not honoured with candles, not adorned with silk, not adored with invocation for the purpose of obtaining help, not set forth for a special cult. Neither was a pilgrimage instituted to these bones for the purpose of there seeking the grace and power of God; indulgences were not promised; these relics were not laid on the sick and on the dead; people did not swear by them; faith and hope were not placed in them, etc. We read absolutely no such thing in Scripture about the relics of Elisha, also after that outstanding and amazing miracle through his bones had taken place. But the bones of the prophets were left in their tombs or sepulchres, as also Christ declares (Matt. 23:29)." [4]

So, let's reclaim this verse. To borrow a biblical expression, Elisha being dead yet speaks. Elisha's bones declare the Word of the Lord to us, so let's listen to what they have to say. Here are two important things I think we can learn here.

In death, our bodies are still united to Christ.

Salvation isn't just for our souls; we're saved as whole persons. So, at death, Christ doesn't abandon our bodies. It's not a case of our souls flying off to Heaven to be with Jesus, while our bodies are quietly forgotten and no longer of any significance. Far from it! That's why when Christianity came to this country our funeral practices changed: we stopped cremating and started burying because Christians die in the sure and certain hope of the resurrection of the body. Our bodies still belong to Christ after death. Our bodies are still united to Christ after death. And so, our bodies will one day be glorious raised by Jesus from death.

These weren't just some bones now lying in a tomb. The 'real' Elisha hadn't flown off to heaven and abandoned them. They were still Elisha's bones. They were still saved bones. They were still bones united to Christ, resting in the grave till the resurrection. Right at the centre of this story of the bones is the identity of those bones. If they weren't still Elisha's bones, united to Christ, there'd be no 2 Kings 13:21.

The power and ability to perform miracles is found in God, and not in man. And God's miraculous power isn't down to the great merit or virtue of the "man of God" either. Just in case anyone wasn't sure about that, 2 Kings 13:21 makes it very clear.

Elisha was dead. That means he couldn't say any special words. He couldn't pray any special prayers. He couldn't perform any special rituals. So, Elisha didn't do anything powerful to heal the man. Only God could have healed him. Only Christ, to whom Elisha's body remained united, could heal the man by coming into contact with those bones.

Elisha was dead. So, he hadn't done lots of good things that week. This miracle wasn't down to how good he'd been of late. It wasn't to do with any virtue in him or any merit he had somehow accrued before God. He was dead. He couldn't do anything. Only God could. Only Jesus.

Elisha was used by God in a miracle to raise the son of the woman of Shunem which is recorded in the Bible, 2nd Kings 4. (2nd Kings 4: 32)

"When Elisha came into the house, he saw the child lying dead on his bed. So he went in and shut the door behind the two of them and prayed to the Lord."

Elisha regularly stayed in Shunem in an upper room prepared for him by this woman and her husband. One day, while Elisha was at Mount Carmel, the couple's young son died. The woman carried the body of her son to Elisha's room and laid it on the bed (verse 21). Then, without even telling her husband the news, she departed for Carmel to find Elisha (verses 22–25). When she found Elisha, she pleaded with him to come to Shunem. Elisha sent his servant, Gehazi, ahead of them with instructions to lay Elisha's staff on the boy's face (verse 31). As soon as Elisha and the Shunammite woman arrived back home, Elisha went to the upper room, shut the door, and prayed. Then he stretched out on top of the boy's body, and the body began to warm (verse 34). Elisha arose, walked about the room, and stretched himself out on the body again. The boy then sneezed seven times and awoke from death (verse 35). Elisha then delivered the boy, alive again, to his grateful mother (verses 36–37).

These miracles were fore-shadow of how Christ's death and resurrection turned the grave into the passageway to new life.

To us, there is nothing weaker than dead bones, yet 'God has chosen the weak things of the world to put to shame the things which are mighty … that no flesh should glory in his presence' (1st Cor. 1:27,29 – and yes, I know Paul's not talking about dead bones there, but the dead bones illustrate the principle). That's the grace of God in Jesus. It's not down to our great strength and power. No. We're weak. We're powerless. But yet by faith we are united to the one who is the wisdom and glory of God.

The widow of Zarephath's son ***(1st Kings 17:17–24)***

Elijah the prophet raised the widow of Zarephath's son from the dead. Elijah was staying in an upper room of the widow's house during a severe drought in the land. While he was there, the widow's son became ill and died. In her grief, the woman brought the body of her son to Elijah with the assumption that his presence in her household had brought about the death of her boy as a judgment on her past sin. Elijah took the dead boy from her arms, went to the upper room, and prayed, "Lord my God, let this boy's life return to him!" (verse 21). Elijah stretched himself out on the boy three times as he prayed, and "the Lord heard Elijah's cry, and the boy's life returned to him, and he lived" (verse 22). The prophet brought the boy to his mother, who was filled with faith in the power of God through Elijah: "Now I know that you are a man of God and that the word of the Lord from your mouth is the truth" (verse 24).

We know that all true Christians who die will rise again someday, but when? Jesus Himself confirmed Martha's statement that there will be a resurrection *"at the last day"* by not correcting her doctrine, but only her faith. And as far as the types are concerned in this story, *"at the very last day"* would be after the very last day of the thousand-year reign. Howbeit Jesus was trying to show her **"a better resurrection,"** one that she, her sister, or any of us could have acquired in our lifetimes. If you are wondering what type of Christian will have to resurrect last, just turn to the Bible.

Degrees and placement for the resurrection of the DEAD

Believe it or not, according to the Bible there will be those who are saved and died without having time to accomplishing any true "Holy Spirit lead works" like the thief on the cross. But what is "Holy Spirit" lead works?" These works are those works that we do for Christ that are led by the Holy Spirit, not our own spirit. Being led implies following the will of another. For example, a prisoner is led by guards to prison; sheep are led by the shepherd to pasture. To be led by the Spirit is to follow the guidance of the Spirit. It is to be submissive to His will, making His desires the rule of life. He is the commander. We are to obey.

The leadership of the Holy Spirit is essential for every believer. To follow the path of selfishness leads to sin, and to follow the path of law leads to bondage. God has revealed in the life of Jesus Christ and in Galatians that there is a third path – following the Holy Spirit.

In Galatians 5:16 walking in the Holy Spirit defeats sin. And in Galatians 5:18 being led by the Holy Spirit avoids bondage to the law. The only proper path for a believer is the one Jesus modeled, following God in personal relationship through the Holy Spirit.

Romans 8:14 teaches that following the guidance of the Holy Spirit is the identifying trait of the children of God. It is essential for every believer to understand the leading of the Holy Spirit and to submit to Him.

Leading and walking with the Holy Spirit

The first way the Holy Spirit leads is through providential teaching. Jesus promised His disciples in John 16:13 that the Spirit would lead them into all truth. Though this promise applied to the apostolic writing of the New Testament, it applies also to Christians today (1st Corinthians chapters 1 and 2).

In Matthew 10:19-20, Jesus instructed the twelve (12) disciples, when arrested for their faith, not to prepare a defense, but to trust the Holy Spirit to give the right words to say. The Holy Spirit can direct the believer's thoughts and words. Similarly, in 1st John 2:27, John encouraged believers to trust the Holy Spirit to distinguish between truth and error. They are not at the whim of fickle teachers and complex-sounding arguments but have confidence the Holy Spirit who will guide them to the truth.

A second way the Holy Spirit leads is through conscious teaching. For instance, when King David gave Solomon the plans for the temple in 1st Chronicles 28:12, David was conscious that the Holy Spirit had led by putting the plans in his mind, helped him to write them down, then explained the details to David (verse 19). In a similar way, the prophets were "carried" by the Holy Spirit as they spoke their prophecies (2nd Peter 1:21). Then also at the conclusion of the Jerusalem council meeting in Acts 15:28, the participants knew their final decision was the decision of the Holy Spirit. Likewise, Paul was conscious that his own preaching was a result of the Holy Spirit at work (1st Corinthians 2:3-5). The principle is that, when needed, the Holy Spirit can direct the thoughts and give understanding in such a way that the believer is conscious that the product is from the Holy Spirit.

A third way the Holy Spirit leads is by communicating specific commands from God. For example, Jesus was led by the Holy Spirit into the desert for the purpose of being tempted by the devil (Luke 4:1). Similarly, the Holy Spirit told Philip to go to the Ethiopian's chariot (Luke 8:29). The Holy Spirit gave a specific detailed command that Philip could obey.

Another example is when the Holy Spirit spoke up at a prayer meeting and said: "Set apart Barnabas and Saul for me for the work to which I have called them" (Acts 13:2-4). After the commissioning service, the two set out, considering themselves to be sent by the Holy Spirit, not by the church leaders. Then it was at the time Paul's mission trip plans were interrupted by the unexpected prohibitions of the Holy Spirit

(Acts 16:6-7). The Spirit can clearly give direct commands, when necessary.

Especially helpful here is the time the Holy Spirit dramatically instructed Peter to go to Caesarea to visit the Gentile Cornelius (Acts 10:19). Because of Peter's strong conviction to the contrary, the Holy Spirit had to be very clear. Note that the Holy Spirit did not always give commands to Peter. To the contrary, Peter received his guidance to go to Samaria by being appointed to do so by those in authority (Acts 8:14); he went to Lydda as part of a prepared tour (Acts 9:32); and he went to Joppa because of the urgent appeal from Christians there (Acts 9:38). Caesarea? That took a vision, the voice of the Holy Spirit, and a human request (Acts 10:9-24). The principle is that the Holy Spirit will take whatever steps are necessary to lead in a particular situation. A human request alone would not suffice for Caesarea. A vision would be superfluous for Lydda.

How do I know that it the Holy Spirit that is leading me?

From the above examples in Scripture, a few generalizations can be made about occasions when the Holy Spirit gives direct commands.

First, this leading of the Holy Spirit is clear. In every example where God gives a command through the Holy Spirit, the direction is specific and understood. God never mumbles. The Holy Spirit doesn't give out clues. A believer should not worry that he has somehow misunderstood God's special direction. When the Holy Spirit speaks, the hearer knows what He has said.

Second, the commands of the Holy Spirit are personal and only intended for the recipient. For instance, only Jesus was called to a wilderness fasting temptation. This is not to be applied as a domineering position for every believer. Likewise, Paul never considered the warnings the Holy Spirit gave Agabus (Acts 21:11) to be a new command for himself (Acts 20:22-23). The Holy Spirit is to the point and is on time for all directions that He gives.

Note in the storyline of Joseph and Mary's engagement situation. Joseph was right by law to decide to divorce Mary ("being a righteous man", Matthew 1:19), in spite of her story of the angel's visit. It was after God gave personal guidance to Joseph did he change his plans.

These illustrate and specific leading applies to the one who receives the leading personally, and not to others. Don't be in error. When the Holy Spirit wants you to act and complete an assignment, He will let you know at the moment that you are wondering or curious if it is the Holy Spirit's directions.

A third observation is that verbal commands from the Holy Spirit are not the normal Christian experience. For instance, there is no indication the Apostle Paul expected any Spirit-guidance when he planned his mission trip itineraries. Paul simply planned his trips and adjusted, as needed along the way. Only when there was something specific God wanted the Apostle Paul to do, something that Paul would not otherwise plan to do, did God communicate through the Holy Spirit additional guidance to Paul (Acts 16:6-10). So, if a believer receives no special guidance from God, that is no cause for concern. Rather, it is a compliment that God considers that the believer is fully capable of obeying God through proper study of Scripture and application of wisdom. We as Christians cannot live without constantly reading the

Bible for instructions. The Holy Spirit acts as a "stamp" in other words, one in agreement with the Word of God.

A final generalization is that commands from the Spirit often seem unwise. Since guidance from the Holy Spirit is usually not what a person would come up with in his own wisdom, the command often seems unusual or even foolish. For instance, Gideon's military attack with only 300 men and Joshua's strategy of walking around Jericho as a means to conquer it, would both be considered foolish if it were not for God's specific direction. This is what is referred to as "Holy Spirit" lead works. Again, these are works that the Holy Spirit leads you to do for God and for His people.

Now that you have been informed what "Holy Spirit lead works are, let's look at some other ways that placement of the resurrection is made.

Placement during the resurrection of Believers

1. There will also be those who got saved and then basically all but *"buried"* their talents.
2. There will be those like the complainer in the parable below who although saved for many years, did little in the way of "Holy Spirit lead works."

Again, since some are saying that others (dead Christians) will be resurrecting from the dead all throughout the thousand years, I feel I must lean on the Word of GOD here once again:

*"...but the rest of the dead lived **not** again till the thousand years were finished."*

Revelation 20:5

Surely the thief on the cross had no time to get sanctified after accepting the blood, and how many people do you think came to Jesus on their death beds, or cried out as some fatal accident overtook them? Some may even believe these brethren represent the *"eleventh hour"* pickers spoken of in the parable of the laborers, but I believe this just shows us once again it's still our "Holy Spirit lead works" that determine our resurrection order. Either way, whichever resurrection one comes forth in, it must still be listed in the Bible's list of resurrections.

"For this cause many are weak and sickly among you, and many sleep."

1st Corinthians 11:30

Let me give you some more information in explanation of what I previously have stated about the order of resurrection and that there are lists in the Bible of how individuals are resurrected. Now you may not find them in totality as “a list” but what you will find is proof that there are different types of resurrections and different times that people are resurrected and why.

These references come out of Luke - Luke 14:1-14; Php.- Php. 3:10-14; John- John 5:28-29; Rev.- Rev. 20:6 showing that there is a part of the resurrection program that is called:

1. “the resurrection of the just,”
2. the “out-resurrection from the dead,”
3. “a better resurrection,”
4. “the resurrection of life,”
5. “the first resurrection.”

These phrases suggest a separation; a resurrection of a portion of those who are dead, which resurrection leaves some dead unchanged while these resurrected undergo a complete transformation.[5]

At the end of this book I feel that I should give you some insight about what I have just said on the former pages. I will use an Old Testament Scripture to prove my point.

"After two days will he revive us: in the third day he will raise us up, and we shall live in his sight. Then shall we know, if we follow on to know the LORD: his going forth is prepared as the morning: and he shall come unto us as the latter and former rain unto the earth."
Hosea 6:2-3

The verse above is clearly one of the better depictions that is found in the Bible pertaining to what can be called the "**fourth** day" resurrection.

Now Hosea 6:2 does not come right out and mention a ***fourth*** *day* per se, but it's revealed as the natural progression of the verse is carried further. The **fourth** resurrection will not be just for **sinners,** but for **marginal Christians** as well, meaning those that died like the thief on the cross, or what 1st Thessalonians 4:14-16 calls those which *"sleep IN Jesus"* vs. *"the dead in Christ."* Basically, we are talking about someone who went no further than repenting and asking for initial salvation (Ephesians 1:13-14 & Philippians2:12).

It still puts me in awe every time God confirms His Word by opening up one of these *"hidden manna"* stories to reveal *the message within the message*. To start with, there are certain Bible based qualifiers that precede those who will come forth in the *"first resurrection"* from the dead, which same resurrection takes place at the beginning of the thousand year reign (Rev 20:4-6). We are told all others (the remaining dead both saved and sinner) must wait until the ***thousand years*** have ended to resurrect from the dead. However, we are also told there will be some who "resurrect" so to say throughout the next millennium, but these believers will have never died in the first place. These will be the "mystery" brethren who will not *"sleep,"* they will just be "changed in the twinkling of an eye" from corruptible to incorruptible as they too submit to the sanctifying work of the Holy Spirit.

The **fourth** day resurrection is when those that *"sleep in Jesus"* shall arise because it says *"after two days He will revive us, in the third day He will raise us*: Rev 20:4 plus those who remain alive: 1st Thess 4:17 *up..."* Hosea 6:2, yet these last brethren who are only *"sleeping in Jesus,"* must wait after the White Throne Judgement.

This last resurrection is shown in type in Numbers 31:19-24. This resurrection fits right in with the judgment of the *"small and great"* who are mentioned in Revelation 19:5. This resurrection takes place at the time of the White Throne Judgment *"after the thousand years have expired."*

The story of Lazarus really brings to light the existence of the multiple resurrections *("every man in his own order"* 1st Cor 15:23) that are described all throughout the Bible.

Lastly, the main events and types in the story of Lazarus' resurrection seem to deliberately focus themselves around a certain number of days. These *"days"* are ascertained by studying the last-day types of creation, where a **day equals a thousand years**. Thus, if we are to ascribe the first "two-days" in the story of Lazarus to symbolically or represent the first two thousand years after Jesus resurrected (**the dispensation of Grace**), then the other reference to ***"four** days"* in this same story should also be ascribed in like manner, i.e., **four** thousand years since Yeshua, or Christ brought forth the Church.

Very seldom if ever does God change the interpretation or usage of a type in midstream, especially when addressing the same subject matter. This is why I entitled this book “the 4th day.” Although I have given you other reasons surface reasons why Lazarus was raised on the **fourth** day, I wanted to give you a bit more.

Therefore, the question may still arise; why did Jesus have to wait *"**four** days"* to raise this Lazarus from the grave? Was He just too busy at the moment, or was it because the Father wanted to show us the power and the hope that remains for even those who must wait to resurrect at the very last-day of resurrection? There are certain types of people that do this.

BUT WHAT ARE THE “TYPES” OF PEOPLE IN THE STORY OF LAZARUS:

MARTHA

(the one who went to meet Jesus first: the "watching" - wise virgin)

Martha (in this instance) is a type for the wise virgins and "**them** that look for Him" as found in Hebrews 9:28. It says that *as soon* as Martha heard that He was coming (behold, the bride groom cometh), *she* ran out to meet Him. It also says, *"now Jesus loved MARTHA, and her sister, and Lazarus...,"* which seems to imply an order of relationship through type. Additionally, Martha and Lazarus are called by name in John 11:5 but not Mary. Previously I saw this *Martha church* as a perfected Church after the marriage, but God has shown me the "man child" brethren will still be learning obedience during their ministry by the things they too must suffer *("sack cloth and ashes")*, right up until their death & resurrection. This means the Man child/Two Witness brethren would still be considered part of the Elect Church during the great tribulation, but only until they are able to faithfully lay down their lives and become part of the Overcomer Church as found in Hebrews 11:40 and Revelation 11:7

MARY

(who sat still in the house; the Shulamite in Song of Solomon 5)

This intentional portrayal of Mary's unwillingness to come out and meet her Master is really exposing the condition of her heart. It seems most people can only remember Mary as the one *"who has choose the good thing,"* and Martha the carnal thing, but types do change in the Bible. Keep in mind, the *"good"* realm is still the lowest of the three *("that ye may prove what is that good, and acceptable, and perfect, will of God": Rom 12:2).* Obviously in this story Mary must have thought Jesus should have done things differently, and now we see that pride, stubbornness, and self-pity have all taken hold of her.

It seems most of us, if not all, will have to repent of our own fallen natures if we are to ever trust in God's ways over our own. *Offence,* like what Mary had, will keep many from both seeing and obtaining God's perfect will for their lives. Mary is a type for the woman spoken of in Revelation 12 that must flee into the wilderness at the time of the marriage: Matthew 25:10. She is a type of the Shulamite in the Song of Solomon who refused to get out of her bed to meet her beloved: Song of Solomon 5:2-6. Mary would also be a type for the woman that God must protect and preserve through the Two Witnesses during the great tribulation. According to the typologies of 2nd Kings 8:6, some of the *Mary types* will (can) be in the first resurrection but only if they wash their robes in the blood of the Lamb and begin to move as the man child brethren must move during the 42 months. This means they must begin to move in total willing obedience to every command of the Father.

LAZARUS

In this example Lazarus types-out to be one of the saints that must wait until *after* the thousand years have expired (i.e., but the rest of the dead lived not again...). The Bible clearly lays out the reality that some people will get saved but go no further with the process (sanctification, perfection) of deliverance from evil. One of the places this *limited deliverance* situation is shown is in the parable of the seeds, that being there are 30, 60, and 100-fold producers in the household of God. God's intention is that everyone would have come into perfection or completeness during their lifetimes, but we know that's not going to be the case for most. That's because even a Christian with a free-will can have other plans. Coincidently, God has told us there will be different resurrections within the ranks of His Church:

1. 1st: first-fruits;
2. Those changed in the twinkling of an eye from mortal to immortal, and
3. The saints who resurrect at "the last day," the time of the small and great resurrection. Their names *will be*

found written in "the book of life" at the White Throne Judgment.

Sickness not unto death

We know that all true Christians who die will rise again someday, but when? Jesus Himself confirmed Martha's statement that there will be a resurrection *"at the last day"* by not correcting her doctrine, but only her faith. What does that mean, i.e., "at the last day?"

Martha, of course, was Jewish and had been taught from childhood about the resurrection. She had read the resurrection chapter of the Bible, Ezekiel 37. And she was certainly familiar with Job 14:10-12:

" But man dies and is laid away; indeed he breathes his last and where is he? As water disappears from the sea, and a river becomes parched and dries up, so man lies down and does not rise. Till the heavens are no more, they will not awake nor be roused from their sleep."

That did indeed seem far distant into the future. No wonder Martha said: "the resurrection at the last day."

The Pharisees would have agreed with her. They, too, believed in a resurrection at the last day. They would certainly have cited as added proof the prophecy found in Ezekiel 16:44-63. These verses speak of a distant future time of resurrection of the ancient inhabitants of Sodom, Samaria, and Jerusalem.

Jesus had this prophecy in mind when He said, "Assuredly, I say to you, it will be more tolerable for Sodom and Gomorrah in the day of judgment than for that city!" (Mark 6:11). By "that city" Jesus meant one that refuses the message of the Kingdom of God.

Jesus here associated "the day of judgment" with the resurrection at the last day. But if the Jews thought they understood that yet distant future time of resurrection, they and that included Martha certainly they did not understand that there would be an earlier resurrection one that would be a **thousand years** earlier than the one at the last day.

The difference here when Jesus is speaking of the resurrection with Martha's doctrine is that the first resurrection, when Jesus returns at the sounding of the seventh or last trumpet, is a resurrection in which is the one that occurs a thousand years before a second resurrection at the last day. This first resurrection is for those who have become "the work of Your hands," said Job of the Lord (Job 14: 15).

Why is it that the Christian world never can grasp that the resurrection scene in Ezekiel 37 is to mortal life in the resurrection to judgment at the last day? I believe for the simple reason that they assume Jesus Christ was raised in the same body that He died in. (Lazarus was raised in the same body that he died in). Jesus was raised in a spirit being, everlasting God being, with the power to appear as flesh and bone, but whose life was never again to be dependent on breathing air and on the circulation of blood. But the scene in Ezekiel 37 is one of living, breathing beings which are mortals.

Now I am sure you are asking how long will they live as mortals in that resurrection while they are being judged? (Remember, the Church of God in Jesus Christ is composed of those being judged now, as 1st Peter 4:17 tells us, and who will be eternally rewarded after they are judged).

Again how long will they live while being judged? There happens to be only one passage in the prophets which reveals the answer. It is in Isaiah 65:17-25, especially verse 20. We would expect that period to be like the 1,000 years because it is under the government of God, administered by

Christ. This millennial-like prophecy is an immediate prelude to the creation of "new heavens and a new earth" (verse 17).

In verse 20 it states:

"There shall be no more thence (from that time on) an infant of days, nor an old man that hath not filled his days: for the child shall die an hundred years old, but the sinner being an hundred years old shall be accursed."

Several important thoughts are wrapped up in this concise prophecy. Though many infants will begin life anew at that time, there will be no more infants born from that time on. Now there will be family, marriage and love, but no more human reproduction. The aged will begin life anew at that time, but they, too, will fulfill their new span of life.

How long will it be? One hundred years, two jubilee (50-year) periods. That is a good length of time for anyone to learn and live God's ways. Immortality for the righteous!

At the conclusion will be two classes:

1. The Child
2. The Sinner

The last part of verse twenty says: “the sinner being an hundred years old shall be accursed.” They shall be burned up as this old earth melts with “fervent heat” (2nd Peter 3:10). They shall be ashes under the soles of the feet of the righteous (Malachi 4:3). But, who are those spoken of in the expression of “the child shall die an hundred years old?” “The child” is in contrast to “the sinner.”

Let’s look at Luke 18:17 for an answer.

“Assuredly, I say to you, whoever does not receive the kingdom of God as a little child will by no means enter it.”

The prophecy in Isaiah refers to those who become “as a little child” and childlike in humility, openness, and sincerity. “The child” is one who is righteous. How, then, does one understand the expression that “the child shall die?” Because the righteous will not continue to live in the flesh. They shall be given immortality by becoming spirit beings, the eternal son of God, just as the righteous who are alive when Christ returns at His Second Coming:

“Behold, I tell you a mystery: we shall not all sleep, but we shall not all sleep, but we shall be changed in a moment, in the twinkling of an eye” (1st Corinthians 15:51-52).

Notice this: the living righteous, when Christ returns, will not sleep in death, yet they shall die! It is "appointed for men to die once, but after this the judgment." (Hebrews 9:27)

Changed in a moment.

The change from mortal to immortal is a death of the cells of the natural body, but it will happen, "in a moment," as the Apostle Paul said, so one will not even be aware of a loss of consciousness!

Isaiah 65:20 is describing this kind of momentary death, when one is changed to immortality; not the lake of fire, which is the second death, which the sinner who is accursed suffers. So, the great purpose of the second resurrection will be finished in 100 years!

Just be aware that the resurrection of the human race at the last day is a different or second resurrection , one in which multitudes of people rise to live again in the flesh (Ezekiel 37) and "return to their former state" (Ezekiel 16:55). It is for them a time of judgment or trial in which they learn about God's plan for mankind. Also, the book of life is opened to them (Revelation 20:12). They will look back on a thousand years of God's rule and compare it, historically, with the first 6,000 years of human rule under the sway of Satan. They will have to choose, as the few whom God calls today have to choose between God's way or Satan's.

It will be their time of judgment, as today is the time of judgment for God's Church (1st Peter 4: 17). Eternal life will be made available as God's free gift for all who repent and overcome their sinful natures. But for those few who refuse God's ways, their end is described in Hebrews 6:8.

Let's continue our discussion on the types found in the storyline of Chapter 11 of John. And as far as the types are concerned in that story, (Martha's type) *"at the very last day"* would be after the very last day of the thousand-year reign. Howbeit Jesus was trying to show her (Martha) *"a better resurrection,"* one that she, her sister, or any of us could have acquired in our lifetimes. If you are wondering what type of Christian will have to resurrect last, just turn to the Bible. They will be those who got saved and died without having time to accomplishing any true "Spirit lead works" like the thief on the cross.

There will also be those who got saved and then basically all but *"buried"* their talents. And there will be those like the complainer in the parable below who although saved for many years, did little in the way of "Holy

Spirit lead works." Again, since some are saying that others (dead Christians) will be resurrecting from the dead all throughout the thousands years, I feel I must bring to bear the Word of GOD here once again: "...but the rest of the dead lived not again till the thousand years were finished."

Surely the thief on the cross had no time to get sanctified after accepting the blood, and how many people do you think came to Jesus on their death beds, or cried out as some fatal accident overtook them? Some may even believe these brethren represent the *"eleventh hour"* pickers spoken of in the parable of the laborers, but I believe this just shows us once again it's still our "Holy Spirit lead works" that determine our resurrection order.

(Two days – representing the time that the Master went away.)

In the story of Lazarus' resurrection Jesus abode <u>two</u> days in the same place. (at the right hand...) This "two days" is the two thousand years given for the Gentiles to come in. We know that God likens **a day to a thousand years, and visa-versa.** We also know that Jesus came approximately two thousand years ago and has since been *"abiding at the right hand of the Father."* Yet He must return which would be symbolically the *"third day"* from His resurrection. Thus,

Jesus *"abiding two days"* in the same place, speaks of the time where *"the master went away"* until Christ comes back secretly to the remnant Church ("Now Jesus was not yet come into the town, but was in that place where MARTHA met him." (John 11:30; Ps 91:1).

Into Judea again (come into the town)

(the 42 months)

Jesus said, *"let us return into Judaea again,"* but His disciples remind Him how badly they treated Him the first time He was there. Nevertheless, God made a promise to Israel through Jeremiah of which we read of in Daniel chapter 9.

Basically, Jesus/Messiah was to minister to the people of Israel for ***seven*** prophetic years, (seven thousand years) yet we also read in Daniel that He was to be cut off after 3.5 years of that time had expired. Now we are told the Two Witness/Man child ministry receives the other half (42-months) of Jesus' seven-year ministry in Revelation 11 & 12, part of which is used to gather and re-graft natural Israel. It's like the disciples said: *"...remember how they treated you the first time?"* Well, it will be quite different the second time around, for many of them (the Jews) will finally be able to say, *"blessed is he who comes IN the name/nature of the LORD,"* that being the Two Witness/Man child saints. They will be able to say this because God will allow them to be severely attacked and decimated *"until"* they cry out to receive their true Messiah. And when Jesus Himself physically comes back at Armageddon, He will come back as the Lion of Judah to fulfill Isaiah 61:2b and destroy Gog, the horns, and the goats.

In the grave four days

Again, the golden rule applies here in this story: the **four** days Lazarus lies in the grave converts to the fourth thousand year from Jesus' resurrection, just like the "two days" that Jesus "abides in the same place" (at the right hand of the Father) is likened to the approximate two thousand years of the Church age. Thus, I do not believe we can say the "**four** days" in this story converts into the 3.5-days that the Witnesses' dead bodies shall lie in the street in Revelation 11:9; different story, different type. I say this because some have said this fourth day resurrection is a picture of the Two Witnesses resurrecting 3.5-days after they are killed (Rev 11:11), but God is more precise then that my sisters and brethren.

Think of it this way; if someone owes you $4.00 and they say, "Here is $3.50, now we are even!" Would you not say, "Hey, where is the .50¢ that you still owe me?" Thus, **"four"** does not become four, until after $3.99 has been paid. Likewise, the **four** days we are talking about in this story is the time from when Jesus resurrected approximately two thousand years ago, until the "Ancient of Days" sits on His Throne at the White Throne Judgment.

So, these are the ones in the grave that chose not to be in the "first resurrection" by their own free-will. These Christians will have fallen short of the high calling, or they would have come forth at the beginning of the thousand years.

Another thing, many saints from the grave were resurrected after Jesus' resurrection. (Matthew 27:50–53): This is perhaps the most curious of all the resurrections in the Bible because it did not occur at the time of death. Plus, it was not an individual who was raised, but, as the Bible tells, *many* saints (vs 52). We know very little about this group of resurrected saints, other than what the Book of Matthew records: When Jesus gave up His spirit (i.e. Jesus died).

"The veil of the temple was torn in two from top to bottom, and the earth quaked, and the rocks were split."
Mat 27:50-51

Then the "graves were opened," from which "many bodies of the saints who had fallen asleep were raised" (Mat 27:52), "and coming out of the graves after (Jesus') resurrection, they went into the holy city and appeared to many." (Mat 27:53) On the same day Jesus bodily rose from the dead, these saints were also bodily resurrected and became witnesses in Jerusalem to the power of the resurrection from death from our Triune God.

As soon as she heard... the Master is coming

Here is another view of the Son of God, *"the bridegroom's coming."* It says Jesus first came to Martha (a wise virgin) and she went running to meet Him. In other words, she was the one *"watching"* for her Master's return after the two days, not Mary! Mary still abode where she was: Song of Solomon 5:3.

The Master "is" come secretly, after two days, but before the third.

This is a picture of the man-child's birth. It says Jesus first came to Martha outside of the city. It then says Martha went back to her sulking sister to inform her secretly (privately) in the wilderness and told her (Mark 9:9) that the Master has come. This time Mary arises in verse 11:29 and goes to meet Him herself (2nd Kings 8:3).

Bound Hand and foot

Now here we finally come to the whole point of this story. This type of bondage is representative of the condition of those who will resurrect last. These Christians' are all *"bound up,"* but saved! That is to say, they did not receive any or much deliverance in their souls while they lived. As such they come forth or resurrect in that same condition. We see just the contrary to this in the story of the three Hebrews who were thrown into the fiery furnace. Those three (a type of the remnant overcomers) came out of great tribulation unharmed, and yet their bondages were all burned off. Thus, these two groups (the bound and the un-bound) represent the full spectrum of the salvation experience in the household of God.

"And do ye abide without the camp seven days: whosoever hath killed any person, and whosoever hath touched any slain, purify both yourselves and your captives on the third day, and on the seventh day. And purify all your raiment, and all that is made of skins, and all work of goats' hair, and all things made of wood. And Eleazar the priest said unto the men of war which went to the battle, This is the ordinance of the law which the LORD commanded Moses; Only the gold, and the silver, the brass, the iron, the tin, and the lead, Every thing that may abide the fire, ye shall make it go through the fire (1st Peter 4:12; 2nd Peter 3:12,) and it shall be clean: nevertheless it shall be purified with the water of SEPARATION: and all that abideth NOT the fire ye shall make go through the water. And ye shall wash your clothes on the seventh day, and ye shall be clean, and afterward (White Throne Judgement] YE SHALL COME INTO THE CAMP (the camp is the camp of the saints about)."

Numbers 31:19-24

The Gospel of John is one of my favorite books of the Gospels. It is one of my favorites because it is the central theme of the divine Logos, the word that was with God and that was God. This Logos became flesh and dwelt among men in the person of Jesus of Nazareth. John says nothing of a supernatural birth. He regards Jesus as a human being who possessed actual flesh and blood, the same as other people. The most significant thing about Jesus is that the divine Logos was present in him, and all of the marvelous things that he accomplished were by virtue of the power of God. In this way, John conceives the relationship between the divine and the human. Because God was present in Jesus, it is appropriate to refer to Jesus as the Son of God, which is an example of what can happen in the life of anyone else in whom the power of God dwells. In this connection, John says, "Yet to all who received him, to those who believed in his name, he gave the right to become children of God.

The story of the resurrection of Lazarus which is the feature story of this book who is the brother of Mary and Martha, John's interpretation of the signs reaches its climax. Lazarus was dead for **four** days, and at the call of Jesus he came back to life. For John, an event of this kind is a most appropriate symbol of what happens to spiritually dead people when they are receptive to the power of God made manifest in the person of Jesus. This story is found only in the Gospel of John and raises some questions concerning the historicity of the event, for it does not seem at all probable that the authors of the Synoptic Gospels would have failed to relate an event as important as this one if they had known about it. In John's story, he interprets the story, its deeper meaning is disclosed in a statement that Jesus makes: "I am the resurrection and the life. He who believes in me will live, even though he dies; and whoever lives and believes in me will never die."

As Jesus tomb is visited at His resurrection there was fear that evil people must have taken the body of Jesus so must so that when Peter and John discovers the body of Jesus has gone they became somewhat angry. But remember, Jesus was always in control. He did exactly what He said he would do and that was to rise or be resurrected on the third day.[6] Jesus is God in the flesh as the Holy Spirit brings the truth to all of us about Him who was and is our “first-fruit” who was raised from the dead and still lives today.

On the contrary, Lazarus (the Lazarus type of people) are typical of all human beings. Without the indwelling presence of the Spirit of God, all human life is meaningless.

When the Spirit of God enters into our lives, we are no longer dead in a spiritual sense but are partakers of the life that is everlasting.

The 4th Day

Bibliography

1. Edersheim, Life and Times, 699; see also Frederic W. Farrar, The Life of Christ (Salt Lake City: Bookcraft, 1994), 480; D. Kelly Ogden and Andrew C. Skinner, Verse by Verse the Four Gospels (Salt Lake City: Deseret Book, 2006), 452; Jo Ann H. Seely, "From Bethany to Gethsemane," in From the Last Supper through the Resurrection: The Savior's Final Hours, ed. Richard Neitzel Holzapfel and Thomas A. Wayment (Salt Lake City: Deseret Book, 2003), 42.
2. https://www.gotquestions.org/raised-from-the-dead.html
3. https://www.gotquestions.org/raised-from-the-dead.html
4. (Martin Chemnitz, Examination of the Council of Trent, Vol. 4, pp.26-27)
5. J. Dwight Pentecost, Things to Come: A Study in Biblical Eschatology (Grand Rapids, MI: Zondervan Publishing House, 1958), 396.
6. Brown, The Gospel and Epistles of John, 65. Concerning the grave clothes of Jesus, Elder McConkie wrote: "What a picture John has left us of this unique moment in history. Fear fills the hearts of Peter and John; wicked men must have stolen the body of their Lord. They race to the tomb. John, younger

and more fleet, arrives first, stoops down, looks in, but does not enter, hesitating as it were to desecrate the sacred spot even by his presence. But Peter, impetuous, bold, a dynamic leader, an apostle who wielded the sword against Malchus and stood as mouthpiece for them all in bearing testimony, rushes in. John follows. Together they view the grave-clothes-linen strips that have not been unwrapped, but through which a resurrected body has passed. And then, upon John, reflective and mystic by nature, the reality dawns first. It is true! They had not known before; now they do. It is the third day! Christ is risen!" (Doctrinal New Testament Commentary, 1:841–42).